LIFE CHANGING SOLUTIONS THROUGH INSPIRATION

Copyright 2000 by Thomas H. Stephens

D1516733

Contents

Contents

Contents

WHO IS GOD

Who is God? Who is He?
And, why should you believe?
Well, God is Spirit. God is light;
God is faithful. He is right.
He knows our thoughts, words, and deeds.
He knows our sorrows. He knows our needs
He created the world, size and scope.
He created us. He is our hope.
He is wise, sovereign, Holy and just;
Depending on Him is a must.
He is the Alpha; Omega; Lamb and Dove;
A Rock; the Star; Foundation; Love.
He's the Banner; Peace; Lord of Hosts;
God Almighty... who knows the most.
He knows what is and what has been.
He knows the secrets; our untold sins.
He is patient and merciful beyond compare;
His gifts and punishments are always fair.
He's the Creator; Redeemer; Comforter; Teacher;
The Captain; Commander; Shepherd; Preacher.
He's the Bread of Life; Vine; Bishop and Door;
The Judge; Master; Prophet; Lord.
He's the Way...the Truth and the Life;
The Prince; the Power; the Eliminator of Strife.
He's the force on why Jesus was raised.
He is God eternal! Worthy to be praised!!!

WHY JESUS

Jesus had a body...possessed flesh and blood.
He grew; asked questions; always loved.
He hungered and thirsted for righteousness;
Got angry; was tempted; but never missed.
He was weary; tired and sometimes slept;
Suffered; abused and occasionally wept;
Was falsely accused...then crucified.
Was hung on a cross until he died.
But unlike others, His death was planned.
He raised back up to save all men.
For, He was with God at the start;
He gave himself...for this part.
He saw sin...what needed to be done;
So God said "okay," my beloved son."
He came at His appointed time;
To fulfill prophecy; to restore mankind.
He was born to Mary from a spiritual seed.
Price paid in full...to all that believe.
For He is God. God is he;
The saving grace with The Master Key!
Jesus had power over death and disease.
He knew the plots of the Pharisees.
He knew the thoughts of the scribes.
He's worshipped as God, by the wise!
He knew the history of the woman at the well;
He knew what to say and what not to tell.
He was worshipped as God, by many a man;
He healed another with a withered hand;
Changed drinking water into wine;
Healed a leper and the blind.
Healed a man demon-possessed.
Raised Jairus's daughter from her rest.
Fed 5,000 with two fish and bread.
Raised up Lazarus from the dead;
Restored a man's severed ear!
Always faithful. Never feared.
He humbled himself to authority.
Obedient to death so we could be free.
Post resurrection...He reappeared.
To Mary Magdalene said, "I am here."
He appeared to Peter, the disciples and Paul;
500 more even saw.
This guarantee is truly great!
Absent from the body is a Christians fate!

THE HOLY SPIRIT

Went down in the water. Got baptized;
The fog lifted from my eyes.
The Holy Spirit came on me;
Opened my eyes so I can see.
The Spirit came to dwell within;
To teach and restrain me from my sins.
He is God in Act 5:3-4.
He is Eternal Hope forevermore.
The Spirit is part of the Holy Three;
The anointed power that lives in me.
He moves in and out all my veins;
He comforts and protects me in my pain;
He searches, seeks, reveals and finds;
He looks at the heart; interprets the mind.
He prays; directs; often leads;
Convicts; prepares and intercedes.
He loves; grieves and often prays.
The Holy Ghost power clearing the way.
He's the Spirit of God...the Spirit of Christ;
The Spirit that paid the ultimate price;
The Spirit of Truth; glory and grace;
Promise; adoption; holiness and faith.
Miracles; knowledge; mercy; healing;
Wisdom; teaching; giving...fulfilling.
He's the power, left, that dwells within;
To minister to us...to be our friend.
The Spirit came on Moses, Joseph and Saul,
Elisha, Elijah, David and Paul.
He came on them to strengthen and seal;
To assure their plans...to direct and fill.
He is the Spirit that calls and appoints;
Empowers, warns, blesses, and anoints.
The Holy Ghost power...part of the three!
That is why we are free.

THE BATTLE

The battle is tough. The fight isn't done;
But, the war is over. We have won.
The battle is tough. The fight isn't done;
But, the war is over. We have won.
I was a sinner...on the enemy's side;
The field was plentiful; his army wide.
The powerful leader appeared as light;
He captured cities; he conquered by night.
He used his skills with subtleness at first;
Drawn into the excitement...then the bubble burst.
Tricks and traps; many well-laid plans,
To take lost souls; destroy the Holy Land.
It seemed like it would never stop.
Had divide-and-conquer tactics to reach the top.
Economics; race; family and friends.
Division was growing; it looked like the end.
The line was drawn...an all out attack;
The battle seemed lost. Then, Jesus came back.
He came back to give us hope;
To rally the troops; help us cope.
The battle is tough. The fight isn't done;
But, the war is over. We have won.
The battle is tough. The fight isn't done;
But, the war is over. We have won.
Because I was a sinner...now considered a saint,
I still get tired and weary, but never faint.
I work through struggles...trying to do things right;
My mind focused upward...praying for his might;
Asking often to be renewed!
Remembering His promises to see me through.
Protected by his armor...adults and youth;
Breastplate of righteousness; the belt of truth;
Shoes of peace; shield of faith;
Helmet of salvation; the Word's mighty weight.
Now, I'm all dressed up...battled tested each day;
Warrior for Christ...battle-equipped to pray!
Because the battle is tough. The fight isn't done;
But, the war is over. We have won.
The battle is tough. The fight isn't done;
But, the war is over. We Have Won!

LOVE IS

Love is...all that God stands for.
It is suffering; being kind; plus doing more.
It is not being jealous or getting puffed up;
Nor letting personal interests overfill life's cup.
Love is...totally about truth.
It's about hope, compassion and innocent youth.
Love is...giving your all without expecting reward;
It's fighting evil with an iron sword;
It never fails through stress and strain.
Cuts and bruises occur, but it endures pain.
Love is...a bond that cannot be untied;
Continuing to live...even when the body dies.
Love is...all of this and more!
It was seen in the perfect man- Our Father The Lord.

God reached into his Holy Federal Reserve
And paid the price we didn't deserve.
He sent down Grace from heaven above;
Unclean sinners...he showed us love.
He gave His best to save His worst-
Salvation's price for sin's curse.
Salvation through Jesus is a free gift.
Sin weighs us down. God's grace is the lift!
God's grace...God's grace is sufficient for me.
He's my life preserve, on a stormy sea;
My Solid Rock on shifting sand;
My future benefits; my retirement plan.
The stamp and glue on a letter sent;
My food-bread, water...my nourishment;
My life insurance...the HMO.
The starter to my engine; He makes me go.
He's the guiding light directing my path.
A God of love and a God of wrath;
A God of force; a wrecking ball.
He destroys my enemies; He makes them fall.
He's a shovel and plow on a snowy day;
He breaks up the ice; clears the way.
He's the frame; the stand; the picture mount;
My overdraft protection to my Holy account.
My knight in shining armor; my Sherlock Homes-
He solves the mysteries; He protects His own.
He's the umbrella in the midst of rain;
The prescription medicine...to kill the pain.
The on-board pilot with the winning plan.
When others say "No" He says "Can."
He's abundant living; He's abundant life.
The fruits of the spirit; the apple of my eye.
By grace, by grace...I now can see!
God's grace...God's grace is sufficient for me.

SUCCESS

Success. Does that mean you're the very best?
Does it mean you've succeeded without a doubt?
Or, did you do it just for clout?
How did you do it? Get to the top!
Did you step on people without a thought?
Or, did you work hard and follow the good book!
And enjoy the feeling of what it took?
Because, being rich is a poor man's game...
If you don't understand from where you came.
You came from the dust after all ...
When its all over, that s where you shall fall.
Because, on that final Judgment Day;
All the gold and silver will fade away.
All that will remain on that promised afternoon...
Will be your past record...and its coming soon.
So, just remember as you succeed on earth:
Up in Heaven, money has no worth.

OPPOSITES A FACT

Is there an up and down? Day and night;
Sun and moon...black and white;
East and West; North and South;
Right and wrong...confidence and doubt;
Peace...war; love and hate;
Scared...brave; accident and fate.
Helping and hurting; giving and receiving;
Life and death...faithful and unbelieving.
If all these things are believable to you;
If Heaven's above...Hell must be true.
If there is an opposite to every act;
Then, the place below is a definite fact.
And if you want to reach Heaven someday,
Then, come to Jesus. He's the only way.
He is the one who died on the cross;
Shed his blood so we wouldn't be lost.
He paid the price for our sins!
Then, in 3 days He rose again.
He ascended up...to Heaven above.
Dressed in all white, like a precious dove;
And when that final trumpet blows
He's coming back to earth to take the roll.
Those not found in the Book of Life
Will find it hot and not very nice.
But, to those who were faithful to what they had heard;
They will be eternally blessed for following The Word.
But, to those people who didn't believe,
They will suffer eternal punishment and never be free.
So, if you believe that opposites are fact,
Then wake up and listen. Just don't sit back;
For the time is here. Your chance will be lost.
Please hurry now, because it's too high a cost.
Please get moving...not tonight, but today!
Make the right decision. Walk the Christian way!

PARADISE

Paradise on earth will be a beautiful thing!
Blue skies, green grass...yellow flowers, white springs.
The house will sit by the ocean front.
The garden will be plentiful; no need to hunt.
No concrete buildings or iron walls.
Just beautiful landmarks that stand so tall.
Kids of all races...together as one.
People loving each other...making life so fun.
That is what Paradise shall be about.
True freedom of man; no need to doubt.
That is what Paradise shall be all about.
Praising the Lord...no need to doubt.
The day is coming! There'll be no more pain.
The birds are singing only good things.
People are walking and talking as family or friends;
Even though they just met, they are acting like kin.
No fear of animals. No fear of man...
The way it was intended from our Creator's hands.
Love has opened the iron lock.
The shackles have fallen; the old clock has stopped.
The new clock ticks with grace and joy!
I have seen the Light. Now there is no void.
I am filled with the Spirit that boils inside;
Forever given new life. Now I will never die.
That is what Paradise shall be about.
True freedom of man; no need to doubt.
That is what Paradise shall be all about.
Praising the Lord...no need to doubt.
There will be sapphires, emerald, topaz and pearls.
In this Holy City we will dwell.
The streets are paved with pure gold.
Down the center of town the river of life flows.
Fresh fruit in view on each side-
Twelve types in all- from the Tree of Life.
The river flows from God's Holy Throne.
More love, peace and joy then we've ever known.
No sun or moon, no dark of night;
The city gleams brightly with God's Holy Light.
The holy city...crystal clear as glass.
This must be Heaven. We're home at last;
Walking...talking...feeling so fine;
New spiritual bodies, Holy, Divine.
We're home at last; finished the game;
Praising the Lord- His Holy Name.

GOD'S PLAN 4U

When you get down and out
And you begin to doubt...
You don't know right from wrong;
The season is so long.
Just look unto the hill!
Have faith in God's will.
Wait and be still.
Because, God's got a plan for you.
God's plan was from the start.
God's plan-Noah filled the ark.
God's plan-Moses parted the sea.
God's plan-the Hebrew slaves were freed.
God's plan-Jericho's walls came down.
God's plan-Jonah didn't drown.
God's plan-Daniel survived the den.
God's plan-the furnace became a friend.
You must have faith in plans unseen!
You have faith in the water being clean;
Faith in the food restaurants prepare;
Faith in the doctor's care...
Faith in the air you breathe;
Faith in a ship floating on the sea;
Faith that your car will start;
Faith in the pump called your heart;
Faith that an elevator won't fall;
Faith in nature's law;
Faith that a plane will fly;
Faith in the rain coming from the sky.
You must have Faith. You must believe.
Your plans look cloudy, but God can see!
He knows what's best and what's hoped for.
His ways are unknown, but He's the core.
He teaches and guides in His planned path.
He make things right on His behalf.
So, have faith in what God's planned for...
Because, we see in part, but He sees more!

PRAYER POWER

What are prayers really good for?
A lot of times they get ignored!
We ask for things we feel we deserve,
And when they don't come, it strikes a nerve.
The Bible says "Ask and you shall receive."
A lot of people say "Don't believe."
But a prayer is all that you need to say!
Because, God works miracles in His own way.
God tells us that we must pray.
His son-Jesus Christ prayed everyday.
It was often used...way back when.
To defeat evil spirits; to cover our sin.
Prayer saves sinners. It strengthens saints;
Renews our hope, so we won't faint.
It's the right answer...in good times and bad.
The G-O-D connection-whether happy or sad.
It heals, reveals, and glorifies God;
It imparts wisdom, to overcomes the odds.
It's the only cable across the spiritual sea;
The internet link-up to eternity.
It's the petition to our Father's heart;
The ending point AND the start
It's the way to go when you don't know
The answer at life's crossroad.
Do you need power just to make it today?
Then down on your knees and begin to pray.
Do you need power just to make it today?
Then down on your knees and pray!
Pray through joy; pray through pain;
Pray in sunshine; pray in the rain;
Pray above challenges; pray for friends;
Pray at midnight; pray until end.
Pray down strongholds; pray night and day.
Whatever the condition, continue to pray!
Pray for pastor, pray for peace;
Pray for love...that it might increase.
Do you need power just to make it today?
Then down on your knees and begin to pray.
Do you need power just to make it today?
Then down on your knees and pray!

A FLOWER SEED

A flower seed is an amazing thing.
How it is planted in the soil in the midst of Spring;
How it waits to be watered and fertilized;
How the roots and petals come alive;
How it grows and blossoms reaching full bloom.
The flower is potted to brighten the room.
The beautiful flower but, just a seed-
Grows and creates a legacy.
This flower is shaped at home and school.
This flower is known as Y-O-U.
For, your seed goes wherever you go.
Water the soil and you will grow!
Grow in knowledge; grow in truth.
Grow in wisdom...while you're in your youth;
Grow in goodness; grow in grace;
Grow in God, run the good race!
Run it with hope. Run it in peace;
Run it with purpose; never cease;
Reach for the stars; reach to achieve.
The sky is the limit if you believe!
So believe in yourself; believe in your dreams.
Believe in the future; keep your gleam;
Gleam and glow; grasp the prize.
For, just as a flower, you will rise.
You will rise to the top...be kings and queens.
With God as your guide you will reach your dreams!

A REAL MAN

God is searching all over this land.
He is looking for the essence of a real man.
A man that listens and understands;
A man willing to take a stand;
A man willing to love AND cry...
Committed to the truth, not to lies.
A man who takes time to care;
He's guided by faith not by fear.
A man who follows God's Holy Creed.
To educate the youth...inspire and lead.
A man who provides night and day.
In the midnight hour-he gets down to pray.
A man who practices what he preaches;
Studies the Bible-trains and teaches.
A man who's there in troubles and trials.
A man willing to go the extra mile;
A man shaped in the image of God!
He admits he needs his spiritual rod.
He's a lighthouse shining; a beacon of hope.
His eyes are focused on a heavenly scope.
He believes in himself; he believes in the fight-
The struggle to make his community right.
He reflects on the past, but changes today.
He's a man that sees a better way.
He's a man of vision; a man that knows;
A man of action; a man that shows.
A man of purpose; a man that achieves.
A man of God; a man that believes.
A man that rises...higher and higher;
His passion burns a raging fire.
He presses, pushes, and never stops.
He's a man chosen to reach the top.
This man chosen...is one of few.
This man...a leader...called Y-O-U.
So believe in your dreams; believe in yourself;
Believe in the future; the nation's health.
Believe in your purpose; believe it today.
God has chosen YOU to lead the way!

BOOKS OF THE BIBLE

Genesis. Exodus...started it all;
Leviticus. Numbers. Deuteronomy law.
The book of history with Joshua;
Judges. Ruth. Samuel*, Kings*, Chronicles*, Ezra...
Nehemiah worked to rebuild the wall.
Esther saved her people from a fall.
Job. Psalms. Proverbs...gives sound advice.
Ecclesiastes. Song of Solomon...poetry so nice.
Isaiah; Jeremiah; Lamentations-
Shows what happened to the nations.
Ezekiel; Daniel; Hosea and Joel-
More prophetic messages to study and know.
Amos; Obadiah and Jonah-
Preaching warnings; a trip to Nineveh.
Micah; Nahum; Habakkuk-
Repentance and a request sent up above.
Zephaniah spoke; then next Haggai.
The Old Testament ends- Zechariah. Malachi.
The books just mentioned-39 in all;
The next 27 will complete the call.
Matthew. Mark. Luke and John;
Acts. Romans. 1st and 2nd Corinthians;
Galatians. Ephesians. Philippians.
Then comes the book of Colossians.
Thessalonians*. Timothy*. Titus. Philemon;
Hebrews. James. 2 Peters, 1st John;
2nd John, 3rd John...then comes Jude.
The book of Revelation gets us through.
The books just mentioned sixty-six in all;
That completes the Bible call.

* denotes two consecutive books

THE LOTTERY WINNER

There was a man, rich as can be-
Played triple one; hit the lottery.
Left his job...was no loss;
Free at last; he had no boss.
Went and bought a new sport car;
Picked out a mansion. Became a star;
Met a lady... became his wife;
Spent several million to make things right.
Truly happy as can be;
In complete control of his destiny.
Then, a tragic thing happened one unforseen night.
Had a heart attack; hung on to his life.
While laying on his hospital bed,
Relatives wanted his will be be read.
Mattered not that he just might pass;
The bet was-he wouldn't last.
He only lasted an hour or so.
Two days later...he was placed below.
His success, fame, money...all were lost.
His relatives rich; he forget the cost.
His future hopes...now one big fear.
The vapor of life now disappeared!
For all the gold, rubbies, diamonds, and fame;
He would give them back, to forget the pain.
For, he found riches but lost his part.
Forgot to be saved, Jesus, put in his heart.
The control he had...now out of his hand.
He saw the hour glass but not the sand.
The real control was up above-
God the Father his eternal love.
You see, riches are great and fame is fine,
But we're only here a short amount of time.
So play these numbers: choose triple one-
The Father, Holy Ghost, and His Son.

CAN I BE USED

In this day and age, can I be used?
Can't find my purpose, I am a sinner, too.
Drink alcohol; turn my back on my wife.
Hurt a friend; messed up my life.
Now, I'm at the end of my rope.
Nothing left for me. I have no hope.
But, a vision came to me late last night.
Said, faith in Jesus. Put Him in your sight.
Noah got drunk after the flood.
Moses-a slayer-given commandments from above.
David adultery...and that's a fact.
Solomon, was the wisest, and turned his back.
Jonah was a prophet who tried to run.
Abraham doubted the birth of his son.
Peter denied Jesus: told three lies.
Paul persecuted The Church; helped Christians die.
Can I be used in this day?
With faith in God He'll show you the way!
He forgave the saints; He'll forgive you, too.
Repent. Turn back and asked to be used.
For nothing is too big for God to bind.
Just look upward! Put Him on your mind
So, You can be used in this day.
You're the one chosen to show others the way.

WHY GOD

God created the Bible, Heaven and Earth.
He is Spirit person; the Trinity birth.
He is right here; present everywhere.
He knows all things smart beyond compare.
He is omnipotent-power greater than all.
He is God eternal-unable to fall.
He is unchangeable and pure of sin.
He is righteous and fair. On Him you can depend.
He is joy, peace, faith, hope from above;
Kindness, goodness, gentleness, and love.
He created man-one purpose after all-
Body, soul and spirit-to heed to his call!
He gave us the gift of a free will-
To chose to serve Him or to seek after thrills.
Decision first made to take our own path-
Eve and Adam sinned-so God used His wrath.
They were banished; then given work and pain.
The circuit cut; His phone number changed.
They lost connection; spread sin to all.
Made us accountable to His written law.
But, a new cord relinked the line.
Now, falling short doesn't mean being confined.
The remedy for death was given God's loss-
The sinless Jesus died on the Cross.
He is the son of God who paid the price.
Through faith in Him, the dial tone is right!
By confessing with your mouth that Jesus is Lord
And believing in your heart he was raised forevermore,
You are now saved. Cable tied to His tree;
Power hooked up. God...eternally free.
For the Bible was written many years ago,
But instructions still apply. God's in control.!

STOP THE VIOLENCE

What's wrong with people today?
They don't come together; they don't want to pray.
They're wearing blinders as if they don't see...
The poor, the sick, the kids are in need.
Black man, White, Yellow, and Brown,
Take a moment to look around.
See the hurt and grief...see the pain.
Drugs. Guns. Violence. All insane.
Stop the violence. Stop it now.
If we don't stop the violence, all of us will drown.
Change our ways. Look North and South;
Put a positive message in their mouth!
Let them know that we still care.
Led by the Spirit...break the fear.
Stop the violence. Stop it now.
The boat is sinking. It's going down.
But if we try...if we dare;
We can plug the leaks of despair!
Use the tools given us by God–
The sword of the Word, the spiritual rod.
Put the excuses back on the shelf;
Thinking of each other not thinking of self.
Working together...hand in hand;
Guiding the boat under the captains plan.
Stop the violence. Stop it now.
If we don't stop the violence all of us will drown.
Stop the violence. Stop it now.
The boat is sinking. We must turnaround!

REFLECTION

Did you wake up this morning to see a new day?
Did you look into the mirror to see what it had to say?
Did the reflection say that you're the best;
That you worked real hard and rose the ladder of success?
Are your dreams of riches beyond compare?
Did the reflection say, " You have a special flair!"
Is the reflection in the mirror a blinding smoke screen?
Is it the truth...or a dream?
Are you the person that you see?
Is your spirit locked inside...in search of a key?
From the reflection in the mirror you cannot hide.
You can deceive other people but, the mirror doesn't lie.
So, look into the mirror for its powerful view.
Be open to change...so the reflection will be true.

COMMITMENT

Are you commited to do what it takes?
Does your words speak good intentions and your actions make it great?
Do you take the time to do your job right?
Do you work through a challenge with determination and fight?
Commitment is...that force which cannot be taught!
It comes from within...deep in our thoughts.
Commitment is The Difference between first and last!
It's being challenged to the limit; being able to pass.
So, are you committed to do what it takes?
Because, it's not the spoken word, but ACTION holds weight.

WORLD IS SMALL

The world seems big with endless bounds—
Large bodies of water and massive ground.
People speak different languages and live miles apart.
But, we all are human...thus we all have a heart.
You can travel the world in search of a mate,
But love only happens if it is fate.
We all are responsible more than it appears.
We all love and we all share common fears!
We all have emotions and a need for friends.
We live life to the fullest...but it still must end.
We laugh. We smile. We use our minds.
Why is everyone still so blind?

COMPANY IS COMING

Can you see the season? Can you see the time?
God is about to shake mankind!
Something's up. Something's in the air.
Something's changing...so be aware.
God told me to tell all of you,
"The hour's at hand, I'm coming back soon.
I'm coming back to take my own.
I'm coming back to take The Church home."
I'm coming back with the wave of my hand–
A plague of destruction to destroy man.
A blade, a sword, a sifting of wheat;
Cutting off the chaff...with misery and defeat.
A breaking down of honor; a destroying of pride.
The stage has been set. My angels will arrive.
They're in position; they're in the stance.
Come my children while you still have a chance!
The warning has been posted; the writing's on the wall.
I love all people, but evil must fall.
It must fall away...away from me.
Company is coming. Can't you see?
Company is coming, it's moments away.
A twinkling of an eye...maybe today–
Company is coming...so prepare the feast;
My Holy Anointing is being released!
Company is coming...forever more...
I spelled it out in Matthew 24.
Company is coming. I've prepared the way.
Because, this is the day the Lord has made!

ONE ACCORD

One day I was walking in my youth.
Walking down the beach and discovered the Truth.
I discovered a secret written in the sand;
The message was revealed from God's hand.
The message said, "Start right here;
Listen up...open your ears.
Open your hearts...and open your minds."
This message is given to save mankind.
The message is simple and very clear;
This message is one that you must hear.
For we're all created from one seed-
One Jesus Christ set us free.
One bond of blood; one rich reward;
One right. One truth. One spirit. One Lord.
One freedom land; one Holy God.
One heavenly home; one spiritual bod.
One promise. One prayer. One practice to teach.
One plan of salvation; one day to reach.
One peace; one path; one purpose to know;
One Holy Bible to help us grow.
One grace; one God; on one accord.
One spiritual family-in Jesus the Lord.
So bond together and stick as one;
Just as the Father, Holy Ghost and Son.
I said, "Bond together. Stick as one."
Just as the Father, Holy Ghost, and Son!

THE BRONZE MAN

There was a man with bronze-colored skin;
Wool-like hair; kind of thin.
Used His gifts to heal the sick;
Worked with water; His professions top pick.
Prayed daily and did what He said.
Used His talents so the poor could be fed.
Known to do the impossible tasks;
Always willing to go whenever asked.
He was determined and committed to the mission He was sent.
Friends backed out, but He always went.
This man of vision gave until He died.
On the day of His death, some laughed, some cried.
This gifted man was not ordinary at all;
His history stands...like an iron wall.
This man...a carpenter, priest and friend;
God on earth in human skin.
He walked on the water and calmed the sea.
Gave his life. Set us free;
Healed the sick; raised the dead;
Brought the Book so it could be read.
Fulfilled the Old and revealed the New.
To let us know that faith will do.
Laws and works not a fact;
Grace through Him is the only track.
Doing what is said, not saying what to do...
Spreading the Word. Following the Golden Rule.
This man of truth with bronze-colored skin-
The savior of the world. Jesus, your friend.
He's beloved; anointed; blessed; kin;
Servant; substitute; Good Samaritan;
The branch; the groom; the cornerstone;
The rock and foundation of your home.
The Guide; the Heir; the Physician;
The Refuge from indwelling sin.
The King of Kings; The Holy One;
The Messiah; the Word; God's only son.
He's the help, the hope, Salvation's horn;
The Gift; the Glory; God's firstborn;
The Chief; the Child; the Sickle and Rod;
The root of David...the son of God.
The son of Mary; the son of man;
A second Adam...second in command!
A priest, a rose, the beginning and end.
He's the savior of the world. Jesus, your friend.

THE POTTER'S HOUSE

Sometimes in life...you must go through;
The potter is working His way in to you.
Your money and finances are in a wreck.
You are making it daily...paycheck to paycheck.
You are suffering with trials and many tears;
A broken heart. No one cares.
What is The Potter telling you?
"Depend on my strength to see you through!"
For, God uses trials to make change.
He makes sunshine through the rain.
He shapes your pot...from the heat of fire.
He molds your soul to His desire.
He breaks down and builds up on His potter's wheel.
Then designs and approves with His Holy Seal.
For He sees clay as a crystal glass.
Not a broken vessel, but a spirit to last.
So, smile. Be strong...steadfast each day;
Because God is building a kingdom the Potter's Way.
I said, smile. Be strong...steadfast each day,
Because, God is building His Kingdom...the Potter's Way.

KEEP YOUR FOCUS

I can focus on my neighbor's fine house and car.
I can focus on TV...movie stars.
I can focus on celebrities...fame.
I can focus on athletes-champions of the game.
I can focus on sheroes and heroes gone by;
I can focus on others; keep my eye on their prize.
I can focus on all that I see or...
I can focus on God, the Supplier of my needs.

TEN COMMANDMENTS OF
SPIRITUAL HEALTH

Worship no god, no God but me.
Make no idols to look and see.
Never use the Lord's name in vain.
Keep the Sabbath holy...it must be maintained.
Honor your father and mother Every day.
Kill no man; respect his way!
Commit no adultery...commit to one.
Stealing and lying must not be done.
Envy not your brother's wealth.
These Ten Commandments equal spiritual health.

RUSHING AROUND

Everyone rushes at the dawn of day!
Parents rush to work; kids rush to play.
Birds rush to get fresh sap;
The cat rushes to catch that pesty rat.
The rat rushes...to get some cheese.
The trap rushes shut; he shouldn't have sneezed.
Because we rush so much each hour,
We forget to enjoy life...like smelling a flower.
So take time out to hear the musical sound;
For, life means more than rushing around.

GREENER GRASS

The grass always appears greener on the other side.
But when you get there, it's not very wide.
Not only will you find a pair of new lips;
You probably will soon be dismissed.
By the time you have measured the true cost,
Your wife is gone and your girlfriend you've lost.
So, resist temptation and be thankful for what you've got.
Because, the grass will turn brown on that new love you've sought.

SECRET PLACE

Everyone has a secret place...
Something in your past they cannot erase.
Something hidden in the recesses of your mind;
Something that limits and binds.
Something broken; something deep.
Something that causes lost sleep.
But that something that is binding you...
Is a mental cage...no longer true.
Because, you are forgiven. God is sincere!
His answer to you is, "I love you, dear."

TIME

There is a time for everything.
A time for Winter; a time for Spring;
A time for Summer; a time for Fall.
A time to wait and a time to call.
A time to laugh; a time to cry.
A time to live... a time to die.
A time to go; a time to stay.
A time to stand and a time to lay.
There is a time to lift up...and a time to tear down.
A time for quiet. A time for sound.
A time for hope; a time to heal;
A time to cover; a time to reveal;
A time to listen; a time to speak;
A time for strength; a time to be weak.
A time for war; a time for peace;
A time to begin and a time to cease.
There is a time to gather and a time to cast;
A time to be first and a time to be last;
A time to walk and a time to run.
A time for rest. And a time for fun.
A time for friends; a time for foes.
A time for yes and a time for no.
A time for night; a time for day.
A time to fast; a time to pray!
A time to practice; a time to preach.
A time to perform. A time to teach.
A time for trouble; a time for trials;
A time to be serious...a time to smile.
A time for silence...a time to tell;
A time for sick; a time for well.
A time to work and a time to play.
The time is Now, to do it God's Way!

VISION

Three men started in a 10K race;
They were running at the same pace.
The yards and miles went slowly by.
The distance between them was on the rise.
The one in last began to believe.
He envisioned winning; he could see.
He focused and reached for the highest peak;
He saw the obstacles as opportunities to reach.
He began to press...to renew his strength.
Years of preparation seen as he increased his length.
His strides got wider. He crossed the line.
He won the race in record time.
He finished the race. He finally passed.
The average man first; the swift man last.
The race is not won by the swift or strong...
It is won by the person who's vision is long.
Vision is...striving to reach the peak!
It is seeing sunshine through clouds so bleak.
It is being hurt... and seeing hope.
It's finding strength when it's hard to cope;
It's having a drive to pull you through...
It's taking the path traveled only by few!
It's believing in self when others doubt;
It's taking the detour...off the main route.
It's enduring laughs, skeptics, and pain.
It's seeing profit when others see no gain.
It's truly seeing what others don't see.
It's not what is, it's what might be!
For, vision must come so we perish not.
A plan revealed...a dream sought.
So, dream. Be inspired...travel vision's road.
For, few take this path, but it's paved with gold.

BIBLE OVERVIEW

The Bible was written many years ago;
It was written under God's, direct control.
66 Books. Old and New.
Gives us the history and the future too.
It's the only written revelation...given God to man.
Inspired and written by His divine hand!
Genesis tells of creation and sin;
the flood and...when Israel began.
Exodus was given; the law came around.
Up through Esther...Israel's history written down.
Job through Solomon-information to be wise.
The prophets with messages-Isaiah to Malachi
The New Testament starts: Matthew, Mark, Luke and John.
It presents Jesus Christ...the new light He dawned.
Acts tells of The Church and its infancy part.
The Christian movement...the Apostle Paul's start.
Romans through Jude-letters written and sent;
Instructions on what Christianity meant.
The book of Revelation concludes it all.
The final battle... satan's fall.

RAIN

We are different colors on the outside, but on the
Inside we're the same.
If you understand this fact, then you can enjoy the rain.
The rain comes down from Heaven above and makes the gardens grow.
Just like the pretty daisies, people need to glow.
The difference between the raindrops and the rain in people's hearts,
Is not understanding what causes eternal life, and that's what keeps us apart!
So, next time you see a drop of rain and you begin to doubt,
Remember this simple poem. Because, rain is what life is about!

LIFE IS A WATERFALL

Death is a scary thing...
When people think of death,
They think of pain.
However, they should not be scared at all.
It should be seen as a waterfall.
When you are living, you are at the top.
And death brings you down like a water drop.
But like the water which goes back up,
The human spirit will again erupt.
Eternal life will be received
By those individuals with whom the Lord is pleased.
So, do not fear of that darkened day;
You will again rise to see the Lord's Spiritual Ray.

DON'T JUDGE OTHERS

We judge our brothers for what they've got.
We should look at ourselves...deep in our thoughts.
We don't have the right to pick and choose
The one who has more or the one who should lose,
So, do not be so envious of others...
Because, all men are truly your brothers.

EYES ARE THE GATEWAY

The eyes are the end and the start.
They are the gateway and road map to the heart.
No one can look you in the face
Without their eyes showing the case.
They show love, happiness, sadness and sorrow;
...What today holds and the looks of tomorrow.
They're the light and vision of everyone;
Filling the heart with beauty...making life so fun.
Appreciate the gift of being able to see,
Because your body is a lock and your eyes are the key!

FRUIT OF PATIENCE

I went to a tree for a piece of fruit;
Discovered a secret at its root.
The root revealed a mystery.
The fruit of patience is the key!
Patience at birth; patience to grow;
Patience to learn; patience to know.
Patience...to drive your first car.
Patience...to make it very far.
Patience...to acquire a college degree.
Patience...to be all you can be.
Patience to prosper in the midst of pain.
When all appears stagnate...staying in the game.
Patience to grasp a new high!
Patience to remember...God's by your side.
Patience to stand; patience to see.
The fruit of patience is the key!

THE BIBLE IS COOL

Having parties in the sun
Is real cool, if you're having fun.
But parties aren't what life is about.
If you think so, then check this out!
Growing up is real hard.
But without education you won't get far.
Well, I am sure lots of scholars believe that is true;
But, following the Bible is the essential rule.
The Bible tells the truth about days to come;
It mentions the past and what's been done.
But trying to be a part of the "in crowd"
Will cause you problems...without a doubt.
So be yourself and love God!
Because peace on earth should never be robbed.

YOUR CHOICE

You can choose to be happy. You can choose to be sad.
You can choose to be miserable. You can choose to be glad.
You can choose to smile, day and night.
You can choose wrong. You can choose right.
You can choose to rise. You can choose to fall.
You can choose to heed God's call.
You can choose joy in the midst of pain.
You can choose sunshine. You can choose rain.
You can choose to live. You can choose to die.
You can choose to believe God's on your side.
You can choose to stand. You can choose to see.
The choice is yours...choose VICTORY!

BLACK MAN

Black Man, where did I come from? Am I a good husband and a son?
Black Man, when will I die? I have no feelings and cannot cry.
Black Man, what's the hope for me? My faith in God is the key.
For as a Black Man, I will survive. By trusting in the Lord I will strive!
Society says that I have no hope; It says that my job is selling dope.
But when I glance back over my youth, I find out the unseen truth...
That what Grandma taught was right! God is the key to winning the fight!
For I am a Black Man...not defined by clothes.
I am someone not defined by shows.
I am someone not defined by being cool.
I am someone not defined by acting a fool.
For I'm a Black Man with the spirit in my heart.
It's the spirit of God which shall never part.
For God is the Light which guides my path. He intercedes on my behalf.
He helps me through thick and thin. In Jesus Christ, I have a friend!
For, His Word tells me that I am someone: I am a Black Man...a great father and
son.
Because we're as strong as we want to be, united together we will see.
That purpose in life is what living's about. We must make a difference without a
doubt.
Change the tide in this land...working together, hand in hand.
Seeing the vision...through spiritual eyes;
Believing the unseen will make us rise.
Depending on Our Father's rope,
We will wake up with renewed hope...
Kings and Queens forever more.
Back on top as before.
For I'm a Black Man with the spirit in my heart.
It's the Spirit of God which shall never part.

BLACK WOMAN

A dream...a vision...came to me-
A pretty Black Woman...lovely as can be.
A portrait of beauty; a heart so fine;
Educated by life; a Godly mind.
She dressed to impress; so sharp, so clean.
A special lady. God's Beauty Queen.
Her light reflects years gone by...
Many struggles and trials have made her wise!
She understands love and what it's about;
She knows life's detours and the best route.
She's a garden...the harvest...mother of us all;
She's a sister; a wife; a mother-in-law;
She's a delicate rose; a radiant beam.
Inner strength and beauty-unmatched; unseen.
She's the doctor; the helper; the family maker;
The strength...unity...the caretaker;
The trainer; the teacher; the super glue...
A spiritual rock called Y-O-U.
You are bold; compassionate and full of faith;
Courageous; confident and full of grace;
Intense; beautiful; determined; steadfast.
A selfless leader...always first. Never last.
You are Black, Brown, Tan and Cream;
Uniquely original; uniquely supreme.
You are the hope...the dream...reality seen...
A proud Black Woman, God's Beauty Queen!

TREASURE ON EARTH

Understanding life is the name of the game.
It's a must if you don't want to go insane.
Life is easy to understand.
If you desire to do so, then take My hand.
Some people are giving and some are not...
Expecting more return on what they've got.
But as the Bible tells about acquiring mass treasures—
Don't put them on earth; store them in Heaven.
I know it is easier said than done,
But today could be the start of Heaven's eternal fun.
With peace in the heart...and the Lord at your side,
You will always live and never die!
So, try to remember what life is about,
And...forever keep the Lord's words within your mouth.

APPRECIATE PARENTS

Child of the world do not shed a tear.
You are protected, so never fear.
Your mother and father love you so...
Your stay on earth will be like gold.
You shall shine and sparkle without a doubt...
So, stop that crying and don't you pout.
For, mom and dad will erase your pain;
Remove all troubles and accept the blame.
That is what parents try to do-
Shield their children from earth's evil rule.
Respect your parents and you shall never be robbed
Of the beautiful life given to you by God.

RESPECT THE OLD

Respect the old. They are our kin.
Just like us, they need a friend.
They've experienced life from years gone by.
They offer us much because they're so wise.
Do not ignore the old or push them away.
Respect their feelings each and every day.
For, one day we will be just as old!
And, we'll need a friend...so our story can be told.

FOUNDATION BUILT ON SOLID ROCK

A marriage, just like a house, is only as good as the
Foundation on which it rests.
If it is built on solid rock, then it's probably the best.
If it is built with cheap materials and on sandy soil,
When a storm comes the foundation will uncoil.
Beauty alone is not enough!
The inner person is more important than all the other stuff.
Charm may be false and prettiness vain.
The house looks well-built, but on the inside it is stained.
To build a house that will endure time
Means building a strong foundation with the Bible in mind.

THE FUTURE TO BE

One Sunday I was searching for a game to see.
I came upon a show called The Future To Be!
The show talked about death...and people who rise.
I listened closely; really focused my eyes;
I watched a while...convinced of its truth;
The rapture; the church; the saving of youth.
It explained death...passing into Heaven's light.
Seven years the adversary unleashing his might.
The great false leader...a deceptive mind;
An information network to control the blind.
Destruction. Turmoil. Many will cry.
Some will be saved; many will die.
Then comes the battle- "final game" it's called;
The great last war which finishes it all!
Just when Israel begins to retreat;
A force from Heaven; false leader's defeat.
1000 years. the Millennium rings.
A New Jerusalem. Christ Is King.
The adversary cast into the bottomless pit!
An earthly paradise...God's table we sit.
By Millennium's end many will love Christ.
After that...the ultimate price.
They are judged with the deceiver at the Great White Throne-
Cast into the fiery lake; forever their home.
The new believers in Christ they found.
They're going home; Heaven bound.
They've finished the game; a contract signed.
This story is real. Now is the time!
So look into the Book, and you will see
The unfolding of truth-prophecy.

WEAPONS DON'T KILL

Weapons don't cause war and they don't make people die.
It's caused by the heart of man; the evil in his eye.
You go through various stages of life with weapons in your hands.
But that doesn't bring security. It makes for another isolated man.
So lay down your weapons in America and afar.
Because, the only weapon to win the war is the true gift-
the Spirit of God.

LOVE THY ENEMY

You may laugh at me and hate my color,
But, I love you because your are my brother.
Do what you will; do as you must.
But it bothers me not...even though it's unjust;
For, I've been taught to love...not hate.
This is the key. This is my fate.
So, if you wish to do the same
The Lord will respect you even though you'll suffer pain;
For the pain will cease at the end of time.
Victory will by your. You shall shine.

RELIGION

Why are there so many religions?
With different beliefs and various visions?
Is it because we don't think alike?
Or is it because men wish to fight?
Religion is a powerful tool!
It shows the way...the Golden Rule.
Religious beliefs should bring us together,
Not take us apart like a bird's falling feathers.
So, enjoy religion. It shows the way.
Combined as one, all men shall pray.

MARRIAGE

Marriage can be fun if you take time out
To understand what it is all about.
It is not about white picket fences;
Or even a wife who looks like a princess.
It's about loving one another from the heart;
Considering your partner without a thought;
Fighting the struggle when things seem bad;
Picking each other up when both are sad;
Treating your bodies as if they're one;
That's what makes marriage a lot of fun.
And as you grow old...when time has passed,
You will sit on the porch and smile at the grass.
Because, you understand the meaning of love...
The kind that is sent from Heaven above..

PURPOSE IN THIS WORLD

What is my purpose in this world?
Is it being a fisherman? Catching a whale?
Is it digging a ditch or constructing a wall?
Is it being a doctor? Playing basketball?
What is my purpose? It's hard to say!
But, striving to reach it is the only way.
So, if you work real hard and read the Good Book...
Your dreams will be met when you take a second look.

LORD'S AT HAND

People of the world: The Lord's at hand.
He just wants us to understand,
The time has come for us to change;
To make new meaning of this crazy game.
Life means more than running around;
Making love and painting the town.
It's all about lending a helping hand...
Giving it to your fellow man.
So, if you read closely and follow the lines,
The Bible will take you into the promised times.

PREJUDICE

All men should be the same at heart,
But being prejudiced will keep us apart.
However, there are signs of changes to come.
The new generation has seen the Son.
This Light shines through on darkened nights.
It stops us from feeling so uptight.
Working together...hand-in-hand
Will unite the world and save all men.
It has been written that The Lord will come...
And, if you think about it, you know it's begun.
For, in the end, on those last forsaken days-
We must come together and force racism away.
Because Racism will kill us all.
Not the Russians, the Chinese or a nuclear ball.

THE MASTER'S PLAN

One day I clearly saw God's hand
Holding a scroll titled "The Master's Plan".
It was written in Hebrew and a portion in Greek.
A voice said, "read. It has what you seek"
I began to see God's redemptive plan.
Each line revealed talked about man.
The scroll described the creation of earth;
God in the garden; Isreal's birth;
The separation and sin...a problem to solve.
Genesis 3:15-the issue resolved.
The exodus from Egypt...through the desert sand.
The Jordan River crossing...to The Promised Land.
The prophets speaking, "Thus says the Lord."
The carrying away; twelve tribes by foreign swords;
The repentance; restoration; and coming back home.
God's continued love...because we're His own.
The types of Jesus...so clear to see.
Joseph and David...examples of me.
Moses; Psalms; the prophets explain-
Emmanuel, Son of Man, Messiah is my name.
They said I would come, now I am here.
Victory is won. Death holds no fear.
I am the Slain Lamb. I rose to my feet.
I am the Holy Shepherd watching over my sheep;
I am the Beginning. I am the End.
I am the one who delivers from sin.
I am the blessing. I am the new birth;
I am The Judge, who measures worth.
I am The Truth, the final seal;
The hidden mystery now revealed.
I am the one fellowshiping with man.
God in the garden. The Master's Plan.

THE LIGHT

One day I was sitting by the light;
The hands on the clock said past midnight.
I was sitting there, in my comfortable chair...
Reflecting on why God sent me here;
Reflecting on purpose, strength and might;
Then God said to me. "focus on the light."
He said, it was given the stars and moon;
The light...of sun at high noon.
The light...at the corner directing traffic flow;
The signal saying stop and when to go.
The lights...the stores...the buildings downtown.
The importance of light is all around!
Cars have lights and streets do too.
But the brightest light must shine from you.
For you're God's light...God's light of love.
An Agape light...manifested above.
A shining light...a candlestick;
The Bible's light...Matthew 5:16
You're a light that brightens in a darkened night;
A light that reveals wrong from right.
A light that projects. A light that's fixed;
A light of life that will not mix.
A light that flows; a light that feeds;
A light filled with energy!
So glow with light. You're the light to be.
Increase your light so others can see...
See as Jesus...with anointed sight!
Go cover the world with your God-give Light!

POSITIVE PEOPLE

Positive people have positive lives!
Positive people always strive.
Positive people...full of faith and hope.
Positive people...ability to cope.
Positive people understand
That everything that happens is in God's hands.
Positive people have a positive talk.
Positive people have a positive walk.
Positive people have a positive style.
Positive people have a positive smile.
Positive people go on in spite.
They add up their blessing; they do things right.
Positive people regularly pray.
They are thankful for just one more day.
Positive people have a daily plan.
Their favorite thought is "I can!"
Positive people continue to rise.
They keep their eye focused on the prize.
Positive people continue to believe...
They are destined to achieve!
So think positive thoughts all day long.
Keep a positive voice; sing a positive song.
Be a positive person...the person to be...
And change the world...positively!

SALVATION'S VICTORY

Lord, I am a sinner. I need to be forgiven.
Jesus shed His blood. That's why I live.
He died for my sins...I now repent,
Thanking God for Jesus Christ, he sent.
I now invite Jesus into my heart...
My personal savior; never to depart.
I have finally found a heavenly taste-
God's love, mercy, forgiveness and grace.
I am finally made new. Jesus lives in me.
Death has turned into victory!

PRAISE THE LORD

Praise the Lord every day.
Praise the Lord in every way.
Praise the Lord all day long.
Praise the Lord with a song.
Praise the Lord with a rap.
Praise the Lord with a tap.
Praise the Lord as you talk.
Praise the Lord as you walk.
Praise the Lord as you rise.
Praise the Lord, even if you die.
Praise the Lord when you doubt.
Praise the Lord with a shout!
Praise the Lord with your hands.
Praise the Lord all over this land!
Praise the Lord with your love.
Praise the Lord up above...
Praise the Lord night and day.
Praise the Lord in every way.
Let everything that has breath...Praise the Lord!

THANK YOU JESUS

Thank you, Jesus for food to eat.
Thank You, Jesus for shoes on my feet.
Thank You, Jesus for cloths to wear.
Thank You, Jesus because you care.
Thank You, Jesus for air to breathe.
Thank You, Jesus for eyes to see.
Thank You, Jesus for a strong heart.
Thank You, Jesus for doing my part.
Thank You, Jesus for your guiding hand.
Thank You, Jesus...with you I can.
Thank You, Jesus for bringing me through.
Thank You, Jesus because You knew.
Thank You, Jesus for your mercy and grace.
Thank You, Jesus for the Christian race.
Thank You, Jesus for covering my wrongs.
Thank You, Jesus for giving me a song.
Thank You, Jesus...for a word to preach.
Thank You, Jesus for wisdom to teach.
Thank You, Jesus for anointed speech.
Thank You, Jesus...for the youth to reach.
Thank You, Jesus for passion and drive.
Thank You, Jesus for keeping me alive.
Thank You, Jesus for being a rock.
Thank You, Jesus for not being in a box.
Thank You, Jesus for being sincere.
Thank You, Jesus for faith not fear.
Thank You, Jesus for Matthew 6:33.
Seek You first...and the rest will be.
Thank You, Jesus for a chance to prove.
Thank You, Jesus I'm in love with you.
Thank You, Jesus for dying on the cross.
Thank You, Jesus for paying my cost.
Thank You, Jesus for believing in me.
Thank You, Jesus for setting me free.
Thank You, Jesus...for being the key.
Thank You, Jesus...for Calvary!

FAITH IS

Faith is...believing what others don't believe.
Faith is... seeing what others don't see.
Faith is...being guided by an invisible guide.
Faith is...walking on the uncomfortable side.
Faith is...having a need unmet,
And acting as if it's a sure bet.
Faith is...launching out into the deep.
Climbing a mountain that seems so steep.
Faith is...the ability to believe in spite;
It's being in the dark and seeing the light.
It's having a drive, will to persist.
An invisible force one can't resist.
It's an eye into the future...pressing the past;
It's going forth to complete the task;
It's carrying forward where others might fall.
It's knowing that God controls it all!
It's a servant; a worker; a job well done;
It's completion of purpose; victory won.
It's things unseen but hoped for-
It's the essence of the truth...the Spirit and more.
Faith is...moving by spirit, not sight.
Faith is seeing God's unseen might.
Faith is action. Faith must be.
Faith in the Lord. He's your faithful seed.
He's the Advocate; Almighty; Apostle; Babe;
He's the Carpenter; Deliverer; Author...The Way;
He's a Witness; forerunner; First Fruits; a Friend;
The Savior; Hope; The Beginning; End;
He's the Lion; Meditator; Nazarene; Purifier;
A Rabbi; Ransom; A Refiner of Fire.
He's the Sacrifice; Lamb; Shiloh; Stone.
The Counselor; Prince; Brother; Our Own!
He's the Passover; Potentate; Salvation's Release.
He's the Risen Redeemer; The Anointed High Priest;
He's the payer of debts; the supplier of needs.
He's the faithful Lord...your faithful seed.

GOD'S ROAD HOME

When you travel down the road called "narrow life,"
Directions must be ordered to be precise.
You will travel through valleys-over hills and plains.
Directions fixed-focused; trained.
The path that follows...is the one that leads...
To change the world; to spread God's seeds.
To help the children; to help the kids;
To lead the way to show what is!
A map was given- a divine guide.
You're at the wheel. Teach them to drive,
For they're the ones who will be called
To finish the trip, after all.
The winding roads; the mountains; the hills...
The ones who follow must follow his will.
The will of life; the will to be free;
The will of love...destiny.
The will to believe in answered prayers.
The will to believe God's protecting care.
Belief in truth; belief in light;
Belief in something called "spiritual sight."
Belief that up is better than down.
Belief that blessings will abound;
Belief that you are the one called
To finish the trip, after all.
So believe in the journey; believe in the trip.
Believe in the passenger-His heart-felt tips.
Believe in the road. You're not alone.
You're on the path called God's Road Home!

FOCUS IN

You must focus on the future, not the past.
You must focus on being first, not being last.
You must focus...not on where you've been;
You must focus on the very end.
Focus on the thing that you must do.
Change your thinking...your attitude.
Focus in! for this is it.
Success comes to those who never quit.
Climb the mountain; reach the peak.
Success comes to those who continually seek.
Seek your purpose...your heart's desire!
And change the world with your inner fire.
I said, seek your purpose...your heart's desire .
And change the world with your inner fire!

KING SOLOMON

King Solomon was all he could be.
He searched and sought all he could see.
He was wise and rich beyond compare;
He had mansions...treasure...and many affairs.
He lived large in royal excess!
Finally, he found the secret of success.
Diamonds, gold, rubies; numerous cars;
Education; land; status; stars...
He found it fleeing, except...the end results.
Not making it into Heaven would be his own fault.
And, in the final count...it's all the same.
Success is winning...only, at God's game.
For, everything seen will not last.
The lamp of life will surely pass.
Hopes and dreams will fade away.
Success...measured only on judgment day.
So be successful work hard on earth.
But, place your treasure in true worth.
Be successful. Work hard on earth.
But always remember: who comes first!
Because success is not found in money and fame...
Making it into Heaven is true gain!

YOU ARE BLESSED

Are you homeless?
Are you blind?
Do you have cancer?
Must you sign?
Are you jobless?
Have no friends?
Are you a loser?
You never win?
Have no purpose?
No future to see?
You own nothing?
You have no keys?
You have no health?
You have no hope?
Are you addicted to dope?
You have no bed?
You get no rest?
Then thank the Lord,
You are blessed!

GOD'S PROMISES

God's promises are always right.
His promises are based on divine might.
God has promised you a heavenly home.
He has promised you a name of your own.
He has promised you companionship;
He has promised you fellowship.
He has promised you faith from above;
He has promised you everlasting love.
He has promised you a hand when you need a lift.
He has promised you spiritual gifts.
He has promised you guidance along the way.
He has promised you wisdom to know what to say.
He has promised you strength, power and peace.
He has promised you rest, renewal; release.
He has promised you the right to be called His own.
He has promised you a seat at His throne.
For you are God's child–a saint, a son.
You are first, not last; not loser, but won.
You're the head, not the tail; above, not beneath.
You have victory over that roaring thief!
You are a blessing going in and a blessing going out.
You have dominion without a doubt.
You are divinely chosen to be wise.
You are God's child...on the rise.
So, reflect on promises guaranteed...to be right.
Because, God has promised you a future that's bright.!

THE WILDERNESS

The Wilderness is...where you will find dying.
Where self is purged through lots of crying;
Where broken hearts are broken pieces.
Where the anointing of God slowly releases!
Where the fire is hot; lonely nights are cold.
Fear becomes faith; scared becomes bold.
Where God talks and you listen.
Where sin's tarnish begins to glisten.
Moses-in the wilderness 40 years.
God provided because He cares.
Jesus-in the wilderness 40 days and nights;
Merged with power and might.
Paul in the wilderness-blinded by the light-
Came forth with new spiritual sight.
It's a place where you must be,
In order to set your captives free.
So, free your mind and don't resist.
Accept the training of the wilderness!
Free your mind and don't resist.
The anointing comes from God's wilderness.

BORN TO LEAD

A leader knows what He believes;
How to love and how to please.
How to inspire and motivate;
How to be on time...never late.
How to follow; how to lead.
How to rise; how to succeed.
How to plan, design and create;
How to truly be first-rate.
He prepares; practices and prays each day!
Where others fail He makes a way.
When faced with a problem, trial or test
Others drop out; He shines as best.
He leads through struggles then stands up tall.
He is a leader, after all!
So reach to achieve. Reach for the top;
Never give up! Never stop!
Have faith in God and continue to believe.
Because, YOU were born; born to lead!

BORN FOR GREATNESS

In the beginning, God created you.
There is nothing on earth that you can't do.
You were born with a vision, a purpose, a plan;
Born with creative hands.
Born to love; not be apart.
Born with this truth planted in your heart.
You were born to laugh and born to live;
Born to help; born to give.
Born to know; born to believe;
Born for greatness; born to achieve.
So strive...and expect to succeed.
Because, greatness is your destiny!

GOD IS CALLING YOU

God is calling on the phone.
He is trying to connect to His own.
He is calling you...with the perfect call plan;
Calling out every woman and man.
He is calling You. Said "it's your time."
"Go preach the Word. Change people's minds!"
For the time is short...end coming fast.
"Go reach the lost before time has passed."
You are the salt...a reflective light.
"Go walk in your calling with strength and might."
Be a witness. A witness for Me.
Stop looking at other. You are the key.
For., I called Noah to build a ship.
I called Abraham to take a trip.
I called Moses...set the Hebrews free.
I called Aaron to be the high priest.
I called Joshua...to lead the Israelites.
I called Gideon to defeat the Midianites.
I called Samson to be a strong man.
I called Saul...first king of the land.
I called Solomon to be the most wise.
I called Jeroboam...king of ten tribes.
I called Elijah to warn and preach.
I called Elisha to succeed and teach.
I called John to cleanse and baptize.
I called Jesus to destroy the lie.
I called Paul to spread the Good News.
Now, I Am God, I am calling you.
I am calling you...on the spiritual line.
I am calling you. Said "It's your time."
It's your time to go...go reach the lost;
Go touch their hearts; go explain the cost.
For, the end is coming; the end is near.
Go tell them I love them; that I still care...
But, the end is coming! My promises are true.
That is why I Am God. I am calling you.
I am calling you on the spiritual line.
I am calling you. Said " it's your time."
It's your time to go...go reach the lost.
Go touch their hearts before millions are lost!

SPIRITUAL FOOD

I was hungry and thirsty so, I called the cook.
Asked him for something from his receipe book.
Asked him for some milk, meat, honey and bread.
I was really hungry; wanted to be fed.
So, I went to the restaurant. It was time.
Opened the menu. The food looked fine.
Ate the buffet; and a glass of milk too.
I wasn't full. I wasn't through.
I wasn't filled. I wanted more!
Then the cook came out and suggested The Lord.
For, His food is a special treat–
A full course meal; a spiritual feast.
True milk, true meat, true honey and bread...
The water and food to be fed.
A lamp...a light guiding your path;
The Book of love and a Book of wrath.
A hammer, a fire, a building block;
A solid foundation; a piece of the rock.
A seed, a staff, a powerful sword;
The promise, The Truth, the Book of the Lord.
A compass, a map...directing the trip.
Treasures revealed; eternal tips.
The instruction manual; the teacher's guide.
The book of answers to the question "why?"
Wisdom...strength...power received.
The reference guide to victory!
The books of the Bible...the Bible book.
The key to life. You must get hooked.

WALK THE WALK

People tend to see what they want to see.
People tend to believe what they want to believe.
People tend to talk a lot of talk.
But how many people walk the walk?
Well, I know someone who walked with light.
He walked with power; he walked with might;
He walked with truth; He walked with love.
He always focused on things above.
He continued to walk even after He died;
Destroyed death...never missed a stride.
His name is JESUS, the begotten son.
Our walking example...equal to none.

A WRITTEN PLAN

A written plan will help you succeed.
An inspired goal to reach and achieve.
A view beyond; ahead of the pack.
A definite goal; a definite track.
A gauge; a mark to reach for.
A persistent effort to do more.
A step-by-step account; setting a time;
A strategic map...line by line.
It's following up; seeing it through.
It's having a plan; created for you.
It's developing goals; continuing to believe;
The root and foundation to achieve.
So develop your plans. Set goals today;
Because success is truly just a plan away.

CAN DO IT GOD

God can do it. Yes, He can.
If God can't do it, no man can.
Only God can protect you; hide you in His arms;
Shield you from unseen harm.
Keep you moving when you might quit;
When you need power, He is it.
Only God can take a person feeling down,
And turn the situation completely around.
Only God can take a wrong and make it right;
Turn what appears dark into light.
Only God can take a person feeling low...
Give him joy! He can make it so.
Only God can see what others don't see.
It's not where you've been...it's where you will be.
Only God can do it. Yes, He can.
If God can't do it, no one can.
Only God can do it. Yes, He can.
God does things like no man can!
Only God can do it, because He is, I Am.
He is the one-The Risen Lamb.
He is the guide; the conductor of all;
He is the doctor...always on call.
He is the president; the CEO;
Chief of the universe...in control.
He conducts His will, timely, precise.
He's the sustaining bread, not just a slice.
He inspires His potential...working through you.
If He used others, He can use you too.
For God can do it. He'll do it in spite.
People have agendas. His agenda is right.
His ways are proven; His ways are great.
His timing unknown, but He is never late.
For God is God; no other to call.
He's a Can-Do-It God, after all.

IT IS GOD

It is God who keeps the sun in the sky.
It is God who set the moon on high.
It is God who keeps the stars shining bright.
It is God who gives us day and night.
It is God who divides the land from the sea.
It is God who gives us air to breathe.
It is God who makes our heartbeat go.
It is God who makes our blood flow.
It is God who created our complex mind.
Unlimited universe...we continue to find.
If God is not true, you're an accident!
Do accidents have unique fingerprints?
Listen up, listen up. What's a person to do?
Believe in God. For, God is true.
Listen up, listen up. What's a person to do?
Believe in God. For, God is true!

I AM

I Am God; The Self-Existing One.
I Am the headship over the Son.
I Am Faithful, I Am True.
I Am the Father...watching over you.
I Am Salvation; over Heaven above;
I Am Mercy. I Am Love.
I Am Life. I Am Living.
I Am Help; I Am Giving.
I Am Glory; I Am Strength.
I Am eternity's length...
I Am the key; I Am the lock.
I Am El Sali...God, your rock!
I Am the Staff; I Am the Rod.
I Am El Shaddai...Almighty God!
I Am Jehovah Shalom...the Lord...your peace.
I Am El Olam. I never cease.
I Am Jehovah Chereb; I Am the sword.
I Am Adonai; I Am the Lord.
I Am righteous. That's what I do.
I Am called Jehovah Tsidkenu.
I Am the banner for all to see.
I Am Jehovahnissi.
I Am the healer; I'll bring it to pass.
I Am, Jehovahrophe. My cure will last.
Yes, I Am God. Yes, I Am He.
My names reveal the character of me.
Yes, I Am God. Yes, I Am He.
The Living God...forever to be!

KNOW THE ENEMY

The enemy works on the eyes.
He works on self and pride;
He works on the mind...fills it with doubt.
He says to strive for riches and clout!
He fills your hands with menial tasks;
He keeps on bringing up your past.
He says, "do what you want to do";
Don't worry about others or the Golden Rule.
He says, " be all that you can be,"
Don't go by faith, go by what you see.
Success. Money. Riches and fame...
Life is just one big game!
But...this game leads to the bottomless pit;
Eternal life filled with punishment.
So choose God. Choose God. Choose God today!
For God is life...the only way.

WAKE UP CALL

Beauty. Fame. Riches. Speed.
A champion-always in the lead.
A person of love; a person of truth.
One that captured the essence of youth.
One we truly loved to see;
One full of energy.
One whose time has passed,
But one whose time should have last.
The spirit is living. The body is lost.
We live each day without measuring the cost.
For life is fleeting-a wind over sand.
We think we have time, but it's in His hands.
So, help someone; fulfill your dreams!
Because, life is not what it seems.
It's the spirit that counts; your purpose fulfilled!
For, life is short. This is real!

OVERCOME

Overcoming obstacles is hard to do.
But, if you work real hard, you will come through.
Determination is the key to knocking down walls;
With drive and motivation your obstacles will fall.
If you have a mountain to climb and no rope or shoes,
The battle can be won...if you know what to do.
Reach deep inside or ask for help from a friend.
You must not give up...because you know how to win!

MIND MATTERS

The mind is amazing to understand...
How it releases and binds every woman and man.
How it figures, calculates and thinks;
How It causes you to rise or to sink.
It determines what you think of self;
Controls actions, wisdom and wealth.
It's a well from which life flows;
Feelings. Thoughts. Patterns. Goals.
It gets results...working in you;
Whatever the mind conceives, it can do.
So, focus your mind and concentrate!
For, your mind is the muscle that makes you great!

GIVE NOT TO RECEIVE

Do you know what Christmas is about?
It's not receiving gifts...but giving them out.
Not expecting to act as the chosen one;
But giving your all just to see others have fun.
That is what Christmas is all about–
Giving other people pleasure from handing gifts out!

TEAMWORK

Teamwork is important throughout our lives.
One man cannot win the war...he can only win the fight.
For, if the light glistens upon his face,
It shows that he is a star but the team made him great.
This is a true thought in every facet of life.
Even the President needs a supportive wife.
Glory for one is not glory for all.
But, all for one will destroy any wall.
This key is important to win the war!
Not thinking of yourself will help the team score.

RESPECT

Respect isn't gained by ordering people around.
It is gained by being a teacher, using manners,
And thinking sound.
Living by the Word of God, instead of the opinions of other men,
You will walk the road of happiness...time and time again.
The husband should fulfill his role as outlined in The Book.
But, there are things to headship that must not be overlooked.
You must be self-sacrificing in your love;
For, there is a higher order up in Heaven above.
If you respect your wife, then respect will be returned!
This is expected and should be learned.

EDUCATION

Education is not a privilege it's your right.
If someone tries to deny you, stand up and fight.
Not by throwing punches from your fist;
If you think so, then the point is missed.
The key is to fight with your mind.
You'll win the war every time!
Mind over matter is what they say.
This is truly the only way.
It is going to take a lot of reading books!
But, this is the method not to be overlooked.
If you work real hard...you will achieve your goals.
That is the way to gain real control.

FAMILY CIRCLE

The family circle should produce a tight cling;
Building understanding, compassion, and loving things.
It is the oldest institution that we know of;
The one special unit that is built around love.
However, the family unit has come apart;
Yielding more and more pain from broken hearts.
The counsel that is needed to change this trend,
Is not a psychologist, but the Lord, your friend.
He said, "it is better to give than receive!"
This is the Truth that we must believe.
For the advice of many cannot replace this fact:
That, living by the Bible shall keep the family unit in tact.
The family circle should be preserved throughout time;
Building strength from within...like originally designed.

LAST DAYS

Are we living in the last days?
Where the pretty blue skies begin to turn gray?
Where people are selfish, boastful, conceited?
Children ungrateful, irreligious, disobedient?
Is there unkindness, slander and violent acts?
Only, Love of pleasure and disregard for Biblical Facts?
The outward vision is a blinding smoke screen.
It's up to you regarding what this means.
But, the Truth cannot be hidden under a rock;
For time is ticking on nature's everlasting clock.

MAN'S GIFT

God gave His only begotten son;
For men to live and have eternal fun.
But what happened to this gift?
Did it disappear in the mist?
Is it hidden behind a wall?
Buried deep or behind a waterfall?
No, it is not gone from sight.
Just look in the Bible. It will show you the Light.
For, it is the key to understand
What life beholds for every woman and man.

DREAMING

Dreaming is...a natural gift.
We dream because we need a lift.
Through them we can be a king,
Write a song and begin to sing.
They put us in touch with our mind;
Help us dig deep, search and find.
For, what we have found is not a lie;
It is the truth of our inner cry.
So, go ahead and experience your dreams.
Because it costs nothing and it lets your
spirit gleam.

COMPLAINING

When the summer comes, we wish for snow.
And when snow comes, we complain about the cold.
For some reason, it is never right;
When the moon is out, we wish for sunlight.
When the sun comes out, we complain about the heat;
The blinding rays make us want to retreat.
When it rains outside, we want it to stop.
But when it stops, we worry about our crops.
So, instead of complaining about things we cannot prevent,
Thank the Lord for these precious gifts He has sent.

ANXIOUS

We all get anxious throughout our lives.
Men want to graduate and find a wife;
Little kids get anxious to receive Christmas toys;
Teenage girls get anxious when it comes to boys;
Teenage boys get anxious to get a car
So they can impress that girl they've admired from afar.
The boss gets anxious to see results.
Creditors get anxious when you default;
But being anxious only causes grief.
So...take one step at a time...that is the only relief.

DEFEATED

It really hurts to be defeated.
Sometimes you lose because of being cheated.
Both life and sports have their ups and downs.
This fact of which all men are bound;
However, sometimes losing is a must!
Because, it builds confidence and trust.
For, if you know what the bottom is like,
When you get to the top, you'll handle it right.

THE CAPTAIN

I was called by the captain. He said, "prepare to fly."
I was sitting by the window as the plane began to rise.
As the plane rose to 30,000 feet;
I began to relaxed in my comfortable seat.
As the plane sliced through the fluffly white clouds;
I began to sing; I began to smile.
I began to smile, I began to sing.
For, all the controls were on the Captain's Wings.
The Captain spoke, said look and see;
Now reflect on your past, now think about me.
Now think about what others don't know.
I Am the Captain, I Am in control!

AFRAID

Being afraid is natural to most.
Sometimes you think you've seen a ghost;
But, when you realize it was just your mind.
Those fears will go away in due time.
Fear is so deep; everyone's uptight.
People are so afraid, they won't go out at night.
But, fear can be overcome by all!
Just ask for His help and he will hear your call.

PROTECTED

Are you truly protected behind four walls?
With locked windows and bolted doors–
Scared when someone calls?
Being barricaded in a house is not enough.
It takes trusting the Bible's words;
And, sometimes that is rough.
For on this earth no one is protected from sin.
True protection comes solely from within.

JESUS SAVED MY SOUL

Jesus saved my soul when I was down;
I was lost in sin; now I am found.
He gave me hope when there was none.
He offered me rest from my evil run.
He lightened up my load; showed me the way;
Shined His light through my cloudy day.
Showed His love by the blood He paid.
From a sinner to Christian, now I am saved.
That's why, I love Jesus. Jesus loves me.
Because He set me free.
I love Jesus. Jesus loves me.
Come to Him and you will see!

FRAMED IN LIFE

What do you see in the picture frame?
Family. Fortune. Future. Fame?
A house, a car, or a RV
Look deep in the fame...what do you see?
Do you see success? Do you see the cost?
Do you know what is or what has been lost?
Have you found your purpose...the meaning of life?
Do you sow seeds of peace or seeds of strife?
Look close. Look deep. Visualize.
Your goals framed, actualized.
What has occurred? What will take shape?
An image that is or an image too late?
So develop your picture. It's never to late!
You're a living picture...framed to be great.

GOD'S IN CONTROL

Look to God who sits on high.
In the game of life He cannot be denied.
He's the King of the court. The one to know;
The All-Star God who runs the show.
Up in the sky, without mentioning a word;
He reaches down low; reigns above the birds.
To understand Him is to know the best.
Because He is Holiness.
And if you wish to do the same,
There is a lot more to it than just watching the game.
It takes hard work and perseverance;
Being an example...and praying in the spirit.
But on top of all that fame and gold,
You must know His son who can save your soul.

THE LIFE TRAIN

The train of life goes down the tracks;
Full of steam; full of sacks.
Bags of memories, strength and pain;
Happiness and heartaches fill the train.
Passengers are seated on each side;
Life and death are making the ride.
The train is rolling through city streets;
The engineer positioned in his seat.
A stop at hurt. A stop at health;
A stop at hope. A stop at wealth.
Prosperity; poverty; tracks of peace;
The train keeps moving down the street...
Passing over bridges and through crossing gates,
The train is headed for an eternal date.
Birth. teen. college years;
Marriage. Family. House. Career.
The life train rolls right on through;
Working harder...carrying you.
The train reaches the golden years.
The engineer says, "the end is near!"
The trip has ended...back to the start;
Bags taken off; time to depart.
The passengers get off and return to the dust.
Having a transfer ticket is a must.
The engineer takes one last look...
Checking for names in His transfer book.
The names listed are a special kind;
Pass to Heaven; ticket Jesus signed.
Life is hot. Life is cold.
You can't avoid it. You can't say no.
When you are headed down life's tracks,
Make sure The Engineer has your back.
The life train is about to stop.
Make sure your ticket says " to the top."

GOD GETS THE GLORY

Who sent help when you had a flat tire?
Who saved you from the heat of life's fire?
Who protected you from many things?
Who gave you a song...so you can sing?
Who taught you the meaning of praise?
When you were broke, who gave you the raise?
Who paid the price for you to be free?
Whose words are spoken in your ministry?
Who made a way out of no way?
Who keeps you alive each and every day?
Who dispatched angels when you almost died?
When you were down, who dried your eyes?
Even in the midst of the storm...
When you were separated, who kept you warm?
When you were wading deep in sin...
Who still wanted to be your friend?
You know who it is, you know it is Me—
Now, give me the glory so others can see!

MY BRIDE THE CHURCH

Woke up this morning at quarter past nine;
Heart was aching. Life wasn't fine.
Me and my bride, up all night;
Feelings hurt because love wasn't right.
My bride was wrong but would not give.
Divided house; her ego lived.
I went through the day; my mind thinking back.
My love was complete. Nothing did she lack.
Always showed concern; taking time to pause-
Would give my life for her cause.
Preparation made, gave an easy out.
Saddened by her actions but I didn't shout.
Whenever she was down and in need of a lift;
I kept my vows...gave a special gift.
Tried to please her. What else can I do?
Showed my love...that it is true.
Because I'm in the midst of a holy search;
Looking for love...my bride-The Church.
Said, "I'm in the midst of a holy search."
Looking for love...between saints in the church.
For, I am Lord. I am God;
You can't fool Me with a facade.
I am God. I am Lord;
I'm asking my saints to do more;
For, I am God. I am love;
Remember Me. Remember My Blood!
For, I am God. I am love.
Soon I'm coming back to take The Church above.
So, be concerned. Take time to pause;
Fight together for a just cause!
Pay attention. Don't take the easy route;
I'll guide you in. I'll get you out.
Whenever you are down and in need of a lift,
Remember my Son-my special gift.
Work together. Asking "what can I do?"
Show your love...that it is true.
Because I'm in the midst of a holy search;
Looking for love-my bride-The Church.
Said, "I'm in the midst of a holy search."
Looking for love...between saints in The Church.

FAITHFUL AND TRUE

Have you ever met someone who is faithful and true?
Someone who watches over you;
Someone who is dependable and brave;
Someone who always knows what to say;
Someone who is there when you can't see.
Someone worthy...to believe.
Well, I know someone who is Faithful and True,
Day and night watches over you.
He is the beginning of creation; Dayspring from on high.
The Bridegroom...watching over his bride.
The Holy Child...Abraham's Seed.
The Light of the world...setting captives free.
He's the Minister; The Potter; Jacob's Star.
The Sun of Righteousness sent from afar.
He's the covenant-keeping Prophet; the Appointed Heir;
The Shepherd of the flock guiding with care.
He's the coming Christ; The Ascended Lord.
The Lion of Judah; The Binding Cord.
He a Refuge; a Fortress; a Mighty Light.
He holds things together; making all things right.
His name is Jesus. Faithful and True...
He is faithfully watching over you!

IMMINENT RETURN

Look at what has happened in 100 years.
The Holocaust, wars, Hitler, fear;
Mass production of cars...automobile speed;
The atomic bomb; the cloning of seeds.
Space travel goes
Where we did not know.
Revelations fulfilled;
Great leaders killed...
Kids and gangs rule.
No religion in school.
Easy divorce is the course;
Computer control, economic woes.
Israel makes a Jewish State.
What is the world coming to?
The imminent return of You Know Who!

YOUR WORTH

How much would you accept for your hand or your eye?
What about your leg or thigh?
What about your heartbeat?
How much would you accept for your ankle or your feet?
How much to be confined to a wheelchair?
What about not being able to hear?
What about being on an oxygen tank?
What about dependence on the blood bank?
What about being confined to your bed?
Think for a moment, what has been said!
For what you think really says a lot.
You have been purchased; you have been bought;
Brought with a price; a price to be free.
Your worth valued ETERNALLY.

HOPE

We place hope in friends; we place hope in cars;
We place hope in family; hope in stars.
We place hope in our jobs; hope in our dreams;
Hope in the lottery for all it seems.
We place hope in the bottle; hope in a pill;
We place hope in looks; hope in a thrill.
We place hope in others; a mask...a disguise.
This misplaced hope is not very wise.
For hope is wisdom placed in God's unchanging hand.
He is the hope with the only plan!
So, pass by His water and you will see-
The only hope is God! The Supplier of our needs.
I said, pass by His water and you will see-
The only hope is God! The Supplier of our needs.
For, God gives hope when we want to doubt;
He turns despair inside out.
He uses rejection as a lesson to gain;
He keeps us moving despite the pain.
He pushes us forward, where others won't go;
On the verge of quitting? God says "No."
Grasping the strings of His purple cord...
The Crown of Glory; The Rich Reward.
Reaching the pinnacle; reaching the top...
Hope in Him won't allow us to stop.
So, stand firm in Him and you will see;
He says, "There is no Hope, except for Me."
I said, stand firm in Him and you will see;
He says, "There is no Hope, except for Me!"

MONEY CAN'T BUY TRUTH

As you grow up...you seek money and fame.
You are told that in life...this is true gain.
But this is not what life is about!
Reach inside to resolve this doubt!
Think about what life beholds...
The beauty of love not the riches of gold.

MIRACLE OR NOT

How can a ship stay on the ocean?
It weighs tons and makes quick motion.
Is it because the ship is so small?
Or is it kept floating by an imaginary wall?
It flows through the water like a fish in the sea...
It carries airplanes. Can that be?
What a thought to understand!
It's not a miracle, it's Our Father's hands.

FRIEND

When you are hurting and feeling down;
A friend is important to have around.
Someone who listens and understands
Those big problems like no one else can.
And when a little problem occurs,
That friend is there so you can be heard.
They're by you through thick and thin.
Unlike an associate...they're a true friend.

TRUE HEROINES: OUR WIVES

We must applaud our beautiful wives!
They're the ones who give the gift of life.
Men never seem to realize what they do.
They suffer intense labor pains and still come through.
After it's all over...they never complain;
Even though they're stressed out, they show no pain.
And as the child grows...the mother gives her all.
She works all day and at night remains on call.
Men! Appreciate your beautiful wives!
For, they're the true heroines that bring the gift of life.

BASKETBALL DREAMER

Look at him dance; watch him fly.
When playing basketball he cannot be denied.
He is the king of the court...the one we know;
The mystical man...who is the star of the show.
Up in the sky without mentioning a word;
He reaches new heights...like a human bird.
To understand him is to know finesse...
Because, he is the very best.
And if you wish to be the same-
There's a lot more to it, than just playing the game.
It takes hard work and perseverance;
Being a leader and promoting team spirit.
But on top of all that fame and gold
You must know God within your soul.

STEWARDSHIP

Stewardship is about prayer and praise.
The more we give others; the more we raise.
The more we release; the more we receive;
A spiritual concept. We must believe.
Stewards of God...caring for His land;
Understanding that everything flows from his hands.
It flows downstream from Him to you;
It continues to flow if you know what to do.
Do you give a portion to the sick?
Or do you just cherry pick?
Do you pick the best of the fruit?
Or do you water at the root?
The root ripe in due time;
Blessing others; blessing man kind.
Making a difference; making a way;
The key to God....prayer and praise.
The praise to unlock the financial grip.
Is to understand the concept of stewardship!

THEY SAY

People will laugh and critize you.
They say they can do better what you can do.
They live in the tombs of your pain;
They always speak loss and never gain!
They give excuses, "no way, no how."
They say, "give up...throw in the towel."
But, they are wrong and God is right.
He is the one with all power and might.
So, make a difference follow His will.
A life of purpose...spiritually filled.
Filled with the vision...the Master's plan.
"They say" will be lost. You will stand!

BY MY SIDE

There was a boy; a special friend:
I knew him since way back when.
He had speech problems in elementary school.
God used teachers who knew what to do.
His father, alcoholic, died in his tenth grade.
God was there...to show him the way.
Broken home. Projects a while;
His mom and Sis made him smile.
Moved out of town with a relative,
Apartment was small had a place to live.
He started college...on a grant and a prayer.
The money came somehow; God cared!
He worked at a restaurant; trained to fry and sell.
Burned his hand; God made it well.
His car broke down-starter wasn't right.
He slept in a restaurant...the entire night.
Woke in the morning to a brand new day.
He fixed the starter. God got him on his way.
He messed up his credit; more important to eat.
God was there; got him back on his feet.
He was going down the highway in the midst of snow,
The car spun in a circle; God took control.
He took a vacation. Came back to sob.
His department eliminated; he still had a job.
Hospital sent $10,000 bill.
The money came. God is for real!
Confusion. Worry. Struggles and strife-
God is the Captain directing his life.
He faced a fire, but didn't die!
Because God was by his side.
When you're in troubled don't despair.
God loves you. He will always care.

FAITH IN THE LORD

Combination Poem
Copyright by: Thomas Stephens

Faith is believing what others don't believe.
Faith is seeing what others don't see.
Faith is being guided by an invisible guide.
Faith is walking on the uncomfortable side.
Faith is having a need unmet;
And acting as if it's a sure bet.
Faith is launching out into the deep;
Climbing a mountain that seems so steep.
Faith is the ability to believe in spite;
Being in the dark and seeing the light.
It's having a drive, will to persist;
An invisible force...one can't resist.
It's an eye into the future; pressing the past.
It's going forth to complete the task.
It's carrying forward where others might fall.
It's knowing that God controls it all.
It's a servant; a worker; a job well done;
It's completion of purpose; victory won.
It's things unseen but hoped for;
It's the essence of the truth, the spirit, and more.
Faith is moving by spirit, not sight.
Faith is seeing God's unseen might!
Faith is action. Faith must be...
Faith in the Lord-our faithful seed
He is the Advocate, Almighty, Apostle, Babe.
He is the Carpenter, Deliverer, Author, The Way.
He is a Witness, Forerunner, First Fruits, a Friend;
He is the Savior, Hope...Beginning and End.
He is the Lion, Meditator, Nazarene, Purifier.
He is the Rabbi, Ransom, Refiner of fire.
He is the Sacrifice, Lamb, Shiloh, Stone.
He is the Counselor, Prince, Brother your own.
He is the Passover, Potentate, Salvation's Release.
He is the Risen Redeemer; the Anointed High Priest.
He is the payer of debts; the Supplier of needs.
He is the Faithful Lord-our Faithful Seed.
He is Beloved, Anointed, Blessed, Kin;
He is a Servant, Substitute, Good Samaritan.
He is the Branch, the Groom, the Cornerstone.
He is the Rock and Foundation of your home.
He is the Guide, the Heir, the Physician.
He is a Refuge from indwelling sin.

He is the King of kings, the Holy One!
He is the Messiah, The Word, God's Only Son.
He is the Help, the Hope, Salvation's Horn.
He is the Gift, the Glory, God's firstborn.
He is the Chief, the Child, the Sickle and Rod.
He is the root of David...the Son of God.
He is The son of Mary...the son of man;
He is the second Adam; second in command.
He is a Priest, a Rose, the Beginning and End.
He is the Savior of the world...Jesus your friend.
He is the Alpha, Omega, the Lamb and Dove.
He is a Rock, the Star, the Foundation, Love.
He is the Banner, Peace, Lord of Host.
He is Jesus Christ- who knows the most.
He knows what is and what has been.
He knows the secrets...our untold sins;
He is patient and merciful beyond compare.
His gifts and punishments are always fair.
He is the Creator, Redeemer, Comforter, Teacher;
The Captain, Commander, Shepherd, Preacher.
He is the Bread of Life; Vine; Bishop; Door.
The Judge; Master; Prophet; Lord.
He is the Way, the Truth and the Life!
He is the Prince; the Power; the Eliminator of Strife.
He is the Force; why, you'll be saved.
He is Jesus Christ-worthy to be praised.
He's the Beginning of Creation, Dayspring from on high.
He is the Bridegroom...watching over his bride.
He is the Holy Child...Abraham's Seed.
He is the Light of the world, setting captives free.
He is the Minister, the Potter, Jacob's Star.
The Sun of Righteousness sent from afar.
He's the Covenant-Keeping Prophet, the Appointed Heir.
The Shepherd of the flock, guiding with care.
He is the coming Christ, the ascended Lord;
The Lion of Judah, the Binding Cord;
A Refuge; a Fortress; a Mighty Light.
He holds things together, making all things right.
His name is Jesus-Faithful and True;
Faithfully watching over you.
His name is Jesus-Faithful and True;
Faithfully watching over you!!!!

ABOUT THE AUTHOR

What does it take to overcome obstacles and achieve lasting success? Thomas H. Stephens has the solution. Thomas Stephens is a gifted author, poet, and inspirational speaker who has overcome many obstacles to achieve success. *"What has Thomas overcome?"* He was born prematurely and left the hospital weighing only 4 pounds. He was placed in a special reading program in the fourth grade. His father was an alcoholic. He lost his father to a tragic death while in the 10th grade. His mother, then a single parent, provided for the family. He lived with his grandmother and aunt, before reuniting with his mom and sister in an apartment project in his hometown of Springfield, Ohio. He graduated from high school and move to Columbus with his nephew into a small one bedroom apartment. He started college on a federal grant and worked evenings at a fast food restaurant to support himself. His old car broke down, so he slept in a restaurant the entire night. He messed up his credit. He was faced with many challenges of being married at age 19. While going down the highway in the midst of a snow storm, his car spun in a circle barely missing traffic. His entire department was eliminated while he was on vacation. He was separated from his wife for a year; He was subjected to a voluntary lie detector test; He received thousands of dollars in unexpected medical bills; He faced a life threatening fire and these are just a few of the obstacles he has encountered.

From all these challenges, Thomas discovered that God is the only solution to overcoming obstacles. With God's help, Thomas was able to work for major corporations such as Bank One, Bordens, Chase Bank, and Firstar Bank. He became Assistant Vice President and Director of Community Development for a major financial institution in 1994. While working full-time, he received a duel bachelors degree in finance and business from Franklin University. In addition to this book, Thomas is the author of a workbook entitled *"Financial Control Solutions"* which teaches the principals of basic money management. Thomas also created *"Life Changing Solutions Through Inspiration"* the audio cassette series. Additionally, he created *"Easy Find Bible Rhymes System"* a Bible memorization system. Thomas is a member of the National Speakers Association and has receive numerous awards. He has been featured on the Inspiration Network, Blue Chip Profile, News Channel 4, News Channel 6, The Columbus Post, The Dayton Weekly News and other media.

Thomas lives by the motto, "With God, their is Always Hope;" and with his experience you can clearly see why. Thomas' personal commitment to help others is evidenced by this book. It contains a lifetime of valuable insights that will assist you with a solution to overcome that problem in your life.

Invite Thomas to your next meeting and be inspired and motivated to succeed in spite of the odds. His God-given recall memory of every inspirational piece in this book will make the difference.

Phone: (614) 471-9419
http://www.cincinnati-directory.com/thomas.htm